Genealogy of the

Fenner Family

James Pierce Root

Alpha Editions

This edition published in 2020

ISBN : 9789354027697

Design and Setting By
Alpha Editions
email - alphaedis@gmail.com

[REPRINTED FROM THE RHODE ISLAND HISTORICAL MAGAZINE.]

SKETCH OF CAPT. ARTHUR FENNER, OF PROVIDENCE.

A PAPER READ BEFORE THE R. I. HISTORICAL SOCIETY, MARCH 23 AND APRIL 6, 1886, BY REV. J. P. ROOT.

PLYMOUTH had its valiant Capt. Miles Standish. Providence could boast of its brave and wise Capt. Arthur Fenner. If the former became more noted for his military exploits, the latter was more distinguished for commanding ability in the conduct of civil affairs. The Providence Captain was less hasty and imperious in spirit than Standish, not so quick to buckle on the sword, but he may be pardoned for the possession of a more peaceable frame of mind. He certainly did not seek to make occasion for the practice of his military skill. It is generally admitted that Williams and the other colonists of our own plantation adopted and quite steadily pursued a more liberal and humane policy towards the Aborigines than prevailed in either of the colonies about her. Fenner was not only a soldier, but was possessed of statesmanlike qualities of no mean nature. He was also an expert engineer and surveyor. In his varied relations to town and colonial life he shewed himself a man of admirable genius, with a mind well balanced and sagacious. His comprehensive qualities made him an energetic, shrewd and trustworthy leader in practical affairs. His age, midway between the older and the younger inhabitants, brought him into sympathy with men both of the first and second generations. He deeply impressed himself upon a strangely

mixed community, the members of which, so diverse in
every other sentiment, were drawn together by a common
love of freedom, and by his efficiency and broad common
sense gained for himself a high place of respect and regard.
The Hon. Theo. Foster, who married a sister of Gov. Arthur
Fenner, a great-grandson of the original Arthur, and whose
antiquarian tastes led him to collect genealogical notes of the
Fenner family, conveys the information in his writings, that
Capt. Arthur was of a highly respectable family, and that
he was a lieutenant in Oliver Cromwell's army. This hon-
orable position must have been gained quite early in his career, as he was born in 1622, and as he appeared in Providence in 1649. On the 27th of the 2d month of this year
he was included among the six men for the Trial of Causes,
and on the 3d of the 10th month Robert Williams and
Thomas Harris gave him a receipt in full for his purchase
money, being thirty shillings, he having full and equal right
in the plantation. Those were stirring years in English history between 1643, when Fenner gained his majority, and
the date of his settlement on this side of the water. The
famous battle at Naseby occurred June, 1645, and he may
have taken part in that fight. Three members of this Fenner family were among the early settlers of the town of
Providence, and bore their share of the labor privations and
honors which marked the history of the early founders of
the state. In the year 1646 William and John Fenner, who
are proved by the records to have been the brothers of Capt.
Arthur (and a single record is of more historic value than
many traditions) signed the noted compact in Providence,
promising "to yield active and passive obedience to
the Authority of King and Parliament established in this
colony according to our Charter and to all wholesome laws
and orders that are or shall be made by the major consent of
this town." William Fenner, after a residence of several
years here, removed to Newport in 1659, and from thence to
Saybrook, Conn., where he died, leaving no children, his
two brothers being executors of his will. Capt. John Fen-

ner resided here for a few years, was Town Sergeant in 1657, and among the jurymen in 1660, but finally exchanged his property in Providence with his brother, Capt. Arthur, for land in Saybrook, which last had been inherited by the children of John and Arthur from William Fenner. Capt. John died in 1709, leaving his wife an estate of £500. His only son John died unmarried. His four daughters married respectively into the Palmer, Starkey, Buell and Hazleton families. These "three brothers who came over from England" (*for once* verifying the common, but generally unreliable tradition existing in almost every family), were without much doubt children of Thomas Fenner, an Indian trader, who died in Branford, Ct., May 15, 1647* It was but following the ordinary custom of that period for Capt. Arthur to name one of his first sons Thomas, thus honoring his own father's memory.

PROPRIETORSHIP OF LAND.

His first purchase of property now on record was in 1650, when Nathaniel Dickens deeded him six acres of upland and two spots of meadow. He bought of John Lippitt, of Warwick, in 1652, all his lands in Providence except a five acre lot. From some defaced records, dated about 1654, it appears that he bought of William Barrows, meadow land at Neotaconkonett. In 1657 and 1659 William Field and Richard Waterman, surveyors, laid out the one hundred and fifty acres which he had bought in 1652 of John Lippitt and Hugh Bewitt, bordering on "Newtoconenett", or Pauchasett river, on Tabanapauge pond, and Aushanduck pond, so called by the Indians. Also some fourteen acres on Providence Neck.†

*His inventory included many articles which only an Indian trader would possess, as violet and damask, blue and green and red colored trucking cloths, jews-harps, &c.—[See Conn. Colonial Records.]

†He afterwards increased his farm at Neotaconkanut to 218 acres, his land lying to the south and west of the hill. He settled, however, first near Wackamaquitt Point, on the borders of the Seekonk, having bought the property known as "What Cheer, in 1659, from James Ellis, who two years before had purchased it of Roger Williams. The original deed given by Williams is a characteristic document, in which he speaks of his method and motive of purchase from the Indians. Mr. A. F. Dexter now occupies this property.

Dec. 27, 1664 he was to have the "meere bank, (probably the bluff formerly existing along the river) from the corner of his fence around the point unto a little creek or cove lying next Wackamaquitt Point, on condition of his laying down as much land in another place for towne's use, and also to make three stiles, one by his house, another at the hollow, and another at aforesaid creek, with liberty to people to pass through on foot or upon occasion to land Goods upon said land." From this document it is evident that in 1664 he lived near the Seekonk river, at Waċkamaquitt Point, probably his first place of settlement.*

He received in 1665 a lot in the division of land, and in 1668 some land one-half mile west of "Hunter's Rock."

In 1673 he enlarged his boundaries at Neotoconkonitt, and as late as 1693 purchased three acres salt marsh on the cove on Seekonk river. It is estimated that Capt. Fenner held the title of over five hundred acres of land, including the Neotoconkonitt purchases, and all other lots in Johnston, Cranston and Providence. He was interested as a proprietor, perhaps as one of the heirs of Richard Waterman, in the territory between the Pawtuxet river and the bounds of Providence town, respecting which there was a long and bitter controversy among some of the leading settlers. In 1661 and 1663 Mr. Fenner was appointed one of a committee of three to meet with three Pawtuxet men, with reference to the surveying of lines and fixing of boundaries, and the complications that had arisen, and in 1667 with Roger Williams and Gregory Dexter, he defended the interests of Providence before the Arbitration Court of Commissioners. Confusing questions involving the title, and finally the jurisdiction of Pawtuxet lands were agitated, William Harris being especially active as agent for the Pawtuxet proprietors, and possibly watchful over his own interests.

In 1682 the proprietors made "a loving and mutual agreement to divide all ye foresaid lands equally to all that are

---

*This Wackamaquitt Point has been identified as being near the Red Bridge.

now concerned in the purchase of Pawtuxet aforesaid."
This document was signed by A. Fenner, Stephen Arnold,
Joseph Williams, etc. There was more love in word, however, than in feeling, and the question of jurisdiction had to
be finally settled by the legislation in 1696, and that of the
title was compromised as late as 1712.

Capt. Fenner, before the year 1675,* had left the neigh-
borhood of Wackamaquitt Point and What Cheer, as a place
of residence, and was established in that part of Providence
afterwards included in the town of Cranston upon his
Neotoconkonitt purchases, not far from Gallows' Bridge,
on the Pochasset river. The younger men, like John Steere,
John Sayles, the Winsor, Arnolds, Mowrys and Whitmans
pushed out, some in a northerly and north-westerly direction
into the newly settled districts of the far-reaching township
of Providence, erecting their cabins in the forests, clearing
land, opening highways, building bridges, and becoming the
advance guard of civilization. Capt. Fenner went west
about four miles. The original house, said to have been built
by him in 1662 at this location, was burnt before Jan. 14,
1676,† by the Indians. If it was ever selected as a garrison
house during the Indian wars, to which the terror stricken
inhabitants might flee for refuge from their savage foes,
as tradition affirms, its burning rendered the position untena-
ble, and Fenner doubtless removed to Stamper's Fort, as
his headquarters.

In his letter to the commissioners from the United Colonies assembled at Hartford in 1678, Roger Williams
writes over date of Aug. 25, that year :

"I am requested by my dear friend and neighbor, Capt.
Fenner, of Providence, to be your remembrancer, praying
your Effectual consideration of his case. It pleased the
Most High to stir up the spirit of the noble General Winslow and his army to adventure to pursue the Barbarians in a

---

*As it appears by Roger Williams' letter to Gov. Leverett. Nar. Club
Pub. Vol. 6, p. 376,

†Nar. Club Pub. Vol. 6, p. 379.

(New England) Bitter Winter. Capt. Fenner had lost his
housing and Cattle, but his Stacks of hay (twenty-two) and
his fencing, &c. God suffered the Pagans not to destroy, but
your Army (against their wills) found it necessary to fodder
their Horses and make themselves Lodging with the twenty-
two Stacks, and to make themselves fires with all his fencing,
and with whatever was about the farm Combustable. Capt.
Fenner addressed himself to the Gen'l and Major Treat, and
others of the honourable Gentlemen, who gave some hopes of
some recruits and satisfaction, and so have the Gov. Winslow
and your Gov. Leiverret, (to whom I wrote in this matter) de-
clared their sense that it is unchristian and inhuman that
any one of the King's subjects should (after his great losses
by the Pagans) bear so great a burden alone, to which the
whole Country ought to put the Shoulder. Capt. Fenner (in
hopes of some relief) hath laid his demand so low that it
speaks him wise and moderate and sensible of your Country's Burthens."

We may believe that his ancient house, the ruins of which
still remain, but only as a refuge for the beasts of the field,
was built immediately after the war of 1675-6, probably on
the site of his burned house, nearly opposite to the locality
where the "Red Mill" in Simmonsville now stands, and on
the Cranston side of the road, close by the burial place
where the tombstones of his son Thomas and others of his
descendants may still be found. It has for generations been
known as "Fenner Castle."

Nothing is left of the house as originally built, but the in-
mense and well built chimney about forty feet high and fifteen
feet broad at the base, which is, thanks to colonial masonry, in
a good state of preservation, besides a portion of the decaying
framework, which shows what was the height of the building. The size of the house at first was about twenty feet
square, there being two stories and one room in each story.
Later two or more rooms were added to the house, en-
larging its proportions. No well was ever dug here, but re-
freshing water was drawn from the Oequockomaug (or

Muckamog) Brook running close by. A veteran white mulberry tree, and a huge elm over one hun lred fifty years old, spread their protecting branches near the old ruins. This house was owned and occupied, since the days of Capt. Arthur, by his son Arthur, then by Thomas, son of Maj. Thomas, then by Daniel Fenner the conjurer, and last by Samuel Fenner and his children, Samuel, Benjamin and Polly (who were very peculiar people, it is said) altogether covering a space of one hundred and sixty years from the death of Capt. Arthur down to the death of Polly in 1861. With repairs and paint and proper care, this historic house might have been preserved with its massive timbers as a relic and memorial for future generations to gaze upon with curious interest. Capt. Fenner and wife were taxed in 1687, 15s. and 4d. We may suppose, without much stretch of imagination, that the earlier settlers dreaded taxation, light as it seems to have been, as much as their descendants.

Capt. Fenner, in 1688, reported a rateable estate of 300 acres woodland, 20 acres wild pasture, 10 acres English pasture, 3 acres orchard and meadow, 5 acres planting, with oxen, &c., to all which he quaintly adds as a hint to the assessor: "This is a just account, I pray be not unmindful of the Golden Rule." The landed property of the Capt. was ample, yet there were seasons of scarcity in the new settlement. He had relief granted to him by order of the Council in Hartford, Ct., March 11, 1670, as follows: "Mr. John Fenner had liberty to transport twenty bushels of corn to Rhode Island for the supply of his brother, Captain Fenner."

CIVIL AND POLITICAL LIFE.

Capt. Arthur Fenner was for the greater portion of fifty year in public life, having been one of the principal magistrates of the Colonial Government of Rhode Island, first under the Charter obtained from the Council of State in England in 1644, and afterwards for a number of years, between 1663 and 1689. He occupied the offices of Commissioner for eight years, of Governor's Assistant for nineteen years,

and Deputy for nine years, besides being Town Treasurer
for a short period, and a very frequent member of the
Town Council, of which body he was moderator more often
than any other member, especially at the annual meetings
for the election of officers and the quarterly meetings
where most important business was transacted.

Probably no man was better acquainted with that whole
territory known in the early colonial period as Providence
Plantations, a township including, not only the vicinity of
Providence, but Smithfield, Cranston. Johnston, Scituate
and the other towns to the northern border. His firm, yet
elastic step had trodden the wilderness in all its bridle paths
and Indian trails not only, but through the thickest woods
and underbrush he had pushed his way with eighteen foot
pole or chain, or compass, engaged as he was so constantly
in surveying claims and laying out the rights that had been
granted by the *town.* As early as 1657 he, with others were
empowered "to treat with the Indians that lay claim to the
meadow of Lohusqussuck and clear it for the Towne and
that the above mentioned be accommodated therein."*

In 1659 he was one of the committee "to make out the
western boundary of the colony."†

As a leader of public sentiment Fenner had the good for-
tune to represent the *Rhode Island feeling,* which has always
been exceeding strong. He was for Rhode Island first, last
and all the time. When in 1656-7 Marshal Waite came or
sent from Massachusetts Bay to Warwick to arrest one Richard Chasmore, as the constable and his prisoner were returning through Providence, as night came on they were
compelled to remain at the tavern of Richard Pray before
proceeding with their journey. After the oppressive meas-

---

*Prov. Records, 1657. This tract in Smithfield was afterward called
Louisquissett.

†Rev. E. M. Stone's Burning of Providence,

ures pursued by the Massachusetts government towards the Warwick settlers, the people of Providence were in no mood to allow the slightest infringement upon their rights. The news of the arrest soon spread through the settlement. As the prisoner had been bound over to answer to the Court in this Colony, and as he was no subject of the Bay, and as the constable was not willing to show his authority, it was determined to prevent Chasmore being carried away. The curious old document which narrates this affair brings vividly before us the "personnel" of the hastily assembled town council, not convened by legal warning, but rather under the stress of present necessity and the inspiration of personal liberty. The old record reads:

"Haueinge a commission from authority to goe vnto Pawtuckittsitt for to seaze vppon the body of Richard Chasmor, the which I did: but in our returne backe againe vnto Providence, teakinge vp our quarters that night by reason of the nights approachinge vpon us:* about eight or nine a clock in the night, as wee conseue, there comes in three men, and brought a warrant from Arthors Fenner of Prouidence for to show to the Townes men my warrant or a coppie of itt, but I denied them either for to lett them see my warrant or to giue them a coppie of itt vnless they would lett me know by what power they did demand such a thinge of me: about two howers after or thereabouts comes in Thomas Angell the cunstabel of Prouidence and a sergant with foure men more for to apprehend my body and Rich: Cashmor whoe then was my prisoner for to appere before the townes men that was mett at Rogers Mories, Arthro Fenner sitting in chiefe amongst them: the said Fenner said I in the townes name and with there consent sent a warrant for to see your warrant or a coppie of itt wherein you had seazed the body of Rich: Chasmore but you resisted vnless you did know by what power wee did itt, therefore I haue sent for you in his hineses name to answer for the afront you have put vppon us in takeinge away our prisner from vs: he beinge bound over to answr in or Collinie: then I replied I must say as I sayed before, I desire to know by what power you doe question me whoe am a passenger returninge backe to the bay: desiringe to molest noe other man woman nor child: then rises up one Dexter† and said I desire to speake my consence and to stand for our liberty: Pawtucksitt is in our liberties and not in the bays: William Harris, he said, wee had noe right to seaze a man att Pawtucksitt and if wee had yett wee could not answr what wee had doun for he was there prisner and had given in bayle for to answer in there Colloney: Dexter he stands vp againe and said Mr. President as he is our prisnor I stand for

---

*They stopped at the tavern of Richard Pray, as appears by Sayles' letter.

†The Rev. Gregory Dexter, Pastor of 1st Baptist Church.

our libertye deliuer him to the cunstabl: so herevppon Fenner he com-
manded the constabl to carry him away: Nay saith Dexter thett there be
a mitimus maid and send him to Nue Port prison: wherevppon Fenner writt a mitimus and gave it to the constabl: then seinge they were
resolued to rescue the prisner out of our hands I desired them as they were
Inglish men to give me the grounds of this there rescue the which Fenner
and John Sayls* did promis the which they did and because there were
soe importenat to see my warrant: I tould them I had lett there president
Mr. Williams see itt: What, saith William Harris Roger Williams what is
he he is but our fellow creture and one of vs and hath no more power
than any of vs here, neither shall he although he hath written to the
Gouernor in the bay but wee will call him to an account for his soe doe-
ing, and this he spoke in a slighty and jering manner.

ENDORSEMENT.

Marchal Wait: retour and Rich. Wright's Depos, 1656–57.—Court of As-
sistants, March 1656[7]."   See Hist. and Genealog. Register, 1854, page
293.

The account here narrated brings out the telling points
and the individual traits. Dexter appears as the stickler for
conscience and "our liberty", Harris now as ever, pursuing
Roger Williams with his caustic sarcasm and relentless oppo-
sition, and Arthur Fenner actively controlling the issue.
The Marshal went off without his prisoner, and Roger Williams addressed to Arthur Fenner, as one of the Towne Dep-
uties a "solemn protestation against such disorderly and
dangerous Courses"† assuming his duty as Chief Magistrate
of the colony called upon him thus to protest, and giving
various reasons against the action of the town council.
John Sayles seems to have taken a clearer view of the case
than Williams, as he addressed a very conclusive and pun-
gent letter to the Warwick people, fully justifying the course
taken‡
The commissioners of the United Colonies did not invite
or permit Rhode Island a place in their Councils at this
period, but were quite urgent that she should unite with
them in the persecution of the Quakers, but the Assembly,
through its committee, of which Fenner was one, answered

---

*John Sayles, the founder of the family of this name, married Mary, the eldest
daughter of Roger Williams.

†Printed in R. I. Historical Society Proceedings, 1883-4.

‡See Hist. and Gen. Register, 1854.

the demand by a letter dated Oct. 13, 1657, maintaining the rights of conscience, and shewing the impolicy of persecution.*

Capt. Fenner's political life was not altogether a smooth one. For a period his party fortunes were more or less linked in with those of William Harris, who was a man of the strongest intellectual ability and indomitable will, and who made his power felt at home and abroad, far and wide, but who for the want of a genial spirit and by reason of his obstinacy was continually losing the leadership he had gained. Harris' legal knowledge was extensive and accurate, above that of any of his associates, and a volume of "Statutes in Frequent Use", folio, London, 1661, owned and indexed by him, and afterwards the property of Capt. Arthur Fenner, is in the possession of the R. I. Historical Society. Roger Williams, in a letter dated 1669, refers to Fenner and Wickenden as being among "the many plucked out of the horrible pit in which others yet lay bewitched", (i. e. by Harris) indicating that there had arisen a breach of harmony between them. In the political controversy which divided the town in 1667, and led to the election of two sets of delegates and two sets of town officers, each claiming to be legal, the Fenner party were recognized by the General Assembly, as against the Harris party. Partizan feeling found expression in the statement of the Fenner faction entitled "The Firebrand Discovered", a very caustic document which was sent to the other three towns by the authority of the town of Providence. The counter statement of William Harris was brought before a special session of the Assembly called on complaint of Harris to the Governor, especially to try the case against Fenner. He charged Fenner with making a "rout" in the town of Providence. The controversy, transferred to this body, was for the time being settled rather summarily, by the fining of Harris to the amount of £50,(which sentence was, however, rescinded the next year) and his expulsion from the office of assistant; but the fires

---

*Knowles' Life of Williams, p. 295.

of political discord still lingered in the Providence settlement. We have sometimes complained of the rancour of
party spirit within the period of our observation, but the
quadrennial excitement of our whole country, though on a
wider scale, hardly suggest the boiling cauldron of intemper-
ate partizanship that prevailed in earlier days. A renewed
rivalry arose to the election of 1670 between Fenner and
Harris, and Roger Williams was pressed into the public service on the declination of both, which was a practical victory
for Fenner. The feud re-appeared in 1672, and might have
continued for a much longer period, had not the imminent
danger attending the Indian War of 1675-6, introduced a
more important issue, and united the settlement in opposi-
tion to the common foe.

MILITARY CAREER.

This brings us to the consideration of Arthur Fenner's
distinctively military career in Rhode Island. None will
doubt from the glimpses into his character that have been
afforded us that he possessed

> "The stern self-sacrifice of souls afire,
> For perill'd altars, and for hearths profaned;
> The generous chivalry, which shields the weak."

The history of the colony had been free thus far from the
alarms of war, though the horizon had sometimes been dark-
ened.

The Indian policy which had been practised by the lead-
ers of sentiment in Rhode Island, notably by Roger Williams, had made the native tribes generally friendly with the
colonists, and had it not been for foreign interference and
aggression, much of the sad desolation that swept in the
train of this conflict would have been avoided. But the die
was cast; the struggle was inevitable and fierce. As early
as January, 1676, "Traine bands" having been established,
Fenner, at the head of a force, had a skirmish with one
Joshua Tefft and a few Indians who accompanied him in a
marauding expedition, capturing the former and sending
him to Wickford, where shortly he was executed. Fen-

ner's house "in the woods" at this time, had been burnt.
Providence, so open to the attacks of the infuriated savages,
made application to the General Assembly for protection.
We can understand how Gov. Walter Clark, who at that time
belonging to the Society of Friends, was naturally averse to
all forms of war. Severe criticisms had been passed upon
him, because the assistance needful for the protection of
Providence was not speedily granted. Capt. Fenner smart-
ing under a sense of his losses by the Indians, had joined
freely in these censures, as the Governor addressed him and
his friends a letter, dated 28 day 12 m, 1675-6* which failed
to satisfy the ardent and reasonable desires of the Providence community for the supply of a defensive force. In
this the Governor speaks very temperately of their "evil
suggestions concerning us in authority, especially myself, as
if not worthy to live," intimating that "they might be able
to secure their persons, but for their out-houses he never had
hopes to secure" and plainly informs them of the inability of
the colony to keep soldiers under pay. The Assembly passed
resolutions much in the same vein, speaking of Providence
as an "out-plantation," and inviting the inhabitants of the
same to take refuge in Portsmouth and Newport. Most of
the inhabitants, thus left without hopes of a sufficient military force at home to protect them, accepted the invitation,
as leading to immediate safety, and doubtless were hospita-
bly received on the island, and provided for according to
their need. Some plans of defence, however, at the sugges-
tion of Roger Williams, had meanwhile been carried into
execution. As early as 1656 a fortification of a rude nature
had been constructed on Stampers' Hill, and this at the up-
per end of the "Towne Street," with Wm. Field's house situ-
uated near where the Providence Bank now is, were now
made as secure places of refuge as possible as garrison houses.
Those "who staid and went not away" as the record of the
twenty-eight men reads, must have gathered within these

---

*See Staples, Providence, p. 162.

fortifications when the savages, fresh from the bloody victory over Capt. Pierce and the smouldering ruins of Rehoboth, first made their appearance from the north. Though the details are but few, and the campaign a short one, the scene may be vividly pictured before the mind. Roger Williams, risking his personal safety, crossing the Moshassuck at the ford to meet the red men in the spirit of peace, with the vain hope that he might reason with them as he had formerly done, and induce them for their own sakes to adopt measures of peace. His humane policy rejected, soon after his retiring footsteps, comes the rush of the invading foe, their faggots making quick work with the cabins of the settlement, but the enemy not venturing too near the garrison houses where the brave Fenner and his troops finding it impossible to do more, were waiting an assault in breathless expectation. Most of the houses being laid in ashes, the government consented* to bear the charge of seven soldiers on the colony's account, and Gov. Clark issued a commission dated 19th 4th mo. 1676† to Capt. Fenner as "Chiefe Commander of the King's Garrison at Providence, and of all other private garrison or garrisons there (not eclipsinge Capt. Williams power in the exercise of the Traine Band there, &c.), and have hereby full power and sole command of the souldiers belonging to that garrison." This tender reference to the aged founder of Providence is to be connected with the fact that he had already been appointed a captain in the military service. We cannot think that Fenner did anything or desired to do anything to eclipse the lustre of the great Rhode Island luminary, whose beneficent rays had shone so brightly for so many years upon all around.

---

*In April.

†Dr. H. E. Turner, infers from the fact that Gov. W. Clarke signed Fenner's commission, that the latter was not at this time a convert to the tenets of George Fox. This was his first act as Governor. The Governors of R. I. from 1670 to 1698, except for one year, were members of the Society of Friends, and military commissions or other warlike acts were issued by subordinate officers. [See Newport Hist. Mag. Vol. 1, p. 83.]

Further danger from Indian warfare ceasing within a few months, the officers and men of the King's garrison were discharged from further duty, but the next year on the coming into office of Gov. Benedict Arnold, and the war party, the garrison was re-established with its former officers. Fenner was a member of the Court Martial held at Newport to try certain Indians, and one of those at Providence, who consented to the selling of the captives into slavery. When we consider the great provocation afforded by the loss of their houses and a large share of their personal property we cannot wonder that the colonists adopted repressive, and even punitive measures towards those, who, if suffered to roam at large, might at any time, in the revengeful spirit they were wont to cherish, have inflicted further and serious damage and loss upon the settlers.

That the brave captain was obliged in this campaign to assume responsibilities, for which no settlement was made by the government for some time, appears by a vote of the General Assembly, Oct. 31, 1677, that he should "have one barrill of that powder now in the Commissary, Mr. Wm. Brinley's custody, and the same he is to have in part of pay for the charge of the garrison called the King's garrison at Providence, and if lead bullitts or shott be in the Collony's store he should also have on the same account not exceeding one hundred weight"*

After the war Fenner continued to receive the confidence of his fellow-citizens. In 1678 we read of his choice by the town of Providence "to make his humble Adress, to his majesties much Honor'd Court of the Comitioners from ye Collony Sitting at Boston upon Ajournement ye 23d of this Instant, May and ye sd Towne doth humbly pray the Honor'd Court to vochesafe ye sd Capt. ffenner Creadit and leave to speak and Answer in ye sayd Towne: behalfe as if the said Towne were personally present."

As even New Hampshire attempted to stretch its authority over a part of our little colony, Sept. 10, 1683, he and

---

*Colonial Records, Vol. 3, p. 591.

Peleg Sandford were chosen as "Agents to go to England
as Colony Officers in Regard to Gov. Cranfield of N. Hampshire and the Commissioners who had lately been at Kings
Towne, but would show no commission from the King for
holding Court." It does not appear that the agents went.
Probably the danger of further interference had ceased.

That Capt. Fenner had some legal and literary attain-
ments would appear from his appointment, May 5, 1680, as
a Committee "to put the laws and acts of the colony into
such a method that they may be put in print", as well as in
his appointment in 1687'8 as Justice of the Quarter Sessions and Inferior Court of Common Pleas.

In 1695, July 2, he in company with two others were
chosen by the Assembly to run the northern boundary of the
colony.

FAMILY LIFE.

The household experience of Capt. Fenner, though he
came of a good family, could not have been widely different
from those of the community about him. Life in the early
settlement of the town presented but rude aspects and few
attractions, as we would view them by the standard of our
own age   Narrow accommodations, plain diet with little
variety, continuous toil were the common domestic experien-
ces. The imperious necessities of pioneer life drove the colonists to hard, yet healthy labor within doors and without.
There were no labor-saving machines at hand. The refine-
ments of home according to the modern idea were utterly
wanting. The habits of the people were simple and unos-
tentatious, productive of the rugged virtues that truly adorn
life. The thrifty housewife who presided for many years in
the Fenner home was a daughter of Richard Waterman, Sen.,
one of the earliest settlers with Roger Williams. Her name
was Mehitabel, and she was the mother of six children, (four
daughters and two sons) five of whom were married and
left a numerous progeny. We have no record to tell when
Arthur and Mehitabel were married or at what time she died,

but it is probable that she lived till about 1682 or 3 ; if so, for nearly forty years she "looked well to the ways of her household and ate not the bread of idleness." We may readily imagine the one family room which constituted kitchen, sitting room, parlor, and probably bed room, where the iron dogs in the wide fire place supported the huge logs from which the flames shot roaring up the chimney, and the smoke went curling after, where she who gave "meat to her household and a portion to her maidens", superintended the culinary operations, "strengthening her arms", as the great iron pots were lifted on and off the hooks, and making cooking a fine art by the baking of the Rhode Island Johnny cake. We are captivated by the graceful attitude of the younger Mehitabel as she turns the spinning wheel, and sings in unison with the whirr of its revolution. Young Freelove, too, who afterwards married the Scotch laddie, Gideon Crawford, (a descendant of James Lindsay, 1st Earl of Crawfurd, and a relative of Gov. Cranston) very scripturally "layeth her hand to the spindle and her hands hold the distaff", preparing herself unwittingly to lay her hand to great mercantile enterprises when her husband should have deceased. Phebe or Bethiah spreads the table with the homely feast in the wooden trenchers, or upon the pewter plates, drawing up the wooden settle, and all within are contented and happy. Thomas and Arthur, the boys of the family, when not engaged in the toils of the farm, or in acquiring the rudiments of a good education from William Turpin, the town schoolmaster, were doubtless ranging the wilds, gun in hand, setting the traps beneath, and watching the branches above, anxious to secure the bounties paid for wolf's heads, and squirrel's heads by the town or colony.

Capt. Fenner took for for his second wife, 16th December, 1686, Howlong Harris, daughter of William Harris, formerly his political antagonist, but then [deceased. Her mother, Mrs. Susan Harris, had peremptorily forbidden her marriage with one Mr. Pococke,* but her alliance with Capt. Fenner,

---

*Foster Papers, Vol. 13.

we may hope, was a sufficient honor to give some ease and
comfort to her wounded heart, though she had waited "how
long". That she made an affectionate mother to Capt. Fenner's children, would appear, on the surface, at least, from a
letter addressed by her in the year 1706 to her son Thomas,
after the father's decease, which has come down among the
Fenner papers. This document urges the two sons to immediate action in carrying out their father's wishes, that
they should divide the property inherited from him, and was
evidently written in a very kindly spirit.

Capt. Fenner's last public act, before making his will, was
the signing of a confirmatory deed, on the 25th of December, 1702, alluding to an agreement made in 1688, for the
exchange of land between himself and his brother John, as
as executors of their brother William's estate. His will
was made September 3, 1703, providing for his wife, and
dividing his landed property equally between his two sons,
and he died October 10th of that year. His inventory of
personal property was taken November 2, 1703.*

The tradition came down in the branch of the family
living nearest to the old dwelling place, that Capt. Fenner
cut his initials in a stone which was to be set up at his grave,
and that his children placed it there. A search within a few
years resulted in the discovery of such a stone in the cemetery back of the "Simmons Mansion", near the old house
once occupied by Richard Fenner, son of Maj. Thomas.
On high ground upon the edge of the slope was found a

---

*The inventory of his personal estate amounted to £166 8 0, and
showed him to be a well-to-do farmer, in the possession of five cows,
six calves and four heifers, and abundant farm utensils, while the econo-
my of the household was well represented in the brass kettles, money
scales, warming pan, twelve trenchers and five spoons, with the two
spinning wheels and cards. The library consisted of one great Bible, a
book called statutes, (already mentioned as belonging to William Harris)
and seven small books. The cellar department was thoroughly English,
and stocked with twelve bbls. of cider, two bbls. peach juice, and five
bbls. beere, not to say anything about the twelve empty barrels. Temper-
ance societies were not in existence, and of course had not yet contribu-
ted to the reduction of the number of family cider barrels.

stone with the monogram AF plainly marked. It is also
claimed, however, by others, that this stone marks the grave
of another Arthur Fenner, son of Richard, who died in 1793, and that the
first Arthur was buried in the old cemetery near site of "Fenner
Castle." Mrs. Howlong Fenner died November 19, 1708.

Children of Capt. Arthur and Mehitabel Fenner:

I.   Freelove, married April 13, 1687, Gideon Crawford.
     She died June 1, 1712. He died October 10,
     1707.

II. Bethiah, married Robert Kilton.

III. Phebe, married Joseph Latham. They lived in Say-
     brook, Con. He died 1705.

IV. Thomas, born about 1653; married 1st, Alice Realph;
     2d Dinah Borden. He died February 27, 1718.
     She died December 18, 1761, in her 98th year.

V.   Sarah, buried November 7, 1676.

VI. Arthur, married Mary Smith, daughter of John Smith
     the miller. He died April 24, 1725. She died
     December 13, 1737.

This paper will be followed by other articles, giving an
account of many of the descendants of Capt. Arthur Fenner.

MAJOR THOMAS FENNER'S HOUSE—BUILT 1677.

[From J. A. & R. A. Reid's History of Providence.]

CAPT. ARTHUR FENNER'S "CASTLE."

[From J. A. & R. A. Reid's History of Providence.]

GENEALOGY OF THE FENNER FAMILY.

PAPER NO. 2.

ONE of the interesting peculiarities of genealogical re-
search is the fact that one can never be perfectly satis-
fied that the last storehouse of records relating to family history has been reached. When it might be assumed that
every available source had been diligently sought and drawn
from, every nook and corner explored for old letters and
documents, every drawer rummaged and trunk ransacked, sud-
denly there will turn up from an unexpected quarter new
material which supplements the facts already gained, and
possibly introduces some changes in the narrative hitherto
prepared. Knowing this fact, one is tempted to withhold
the family history from publication, however carefully it
may have been prepared, lest he may be caught by one of
these sudden surprises in some error of statement, but over
against such a possibility must be set the benefits that will
accrue by the issue of the great body of facts, even if some
may afterward be subject to slight corrections. There is always such risk of the destruction of Mss. by fire, that it is
desirable that no one should wait for absolute perfection before committing his work to the press.

Since the publication of the first article on the Fenner
family, an old will has come into the possession of the R. I.
Historical Society, through the favor of Mr. Pardon Fenner
Brown, a copy of which it is our privilege to present here.

It is the original will of William Fenner, probated at Newport, Sept. 6, 1680, as attested by Nathaniel Coddington, Council Clerk, and was the same will, dated Aug. 30. 1680. presented to the Town Council of Providence by Capt. Arthur Fenner on the 5th of January, 1680–81*, although not recorded there. The will does not give his residence, but it was presumably at the time of his death at Newport. Not being a man of family, he may have spent part of his time in Connecticut, where a portion of his property lay, and he was also found at Providence at different periods, where also he had property rights.† From this will it appears that there were two sisters of the Fenner brothers married in this country. One was married to a *Lay* who had died previous to 1680, and was undoubtedly Sarah, first wife of Robert Lay of Saybrook, Conn., who died 21st May, 1676, æ 59, and who was consequently born in 1617, leaving children— Phebe, who mar. 1667, John Denison of Stonington, and Robert Lay of Saybrook, who mar. 22d Jan. 1680, Mary Stanton. The other sister was Phebe Ward, who probably was the wife of the John Ward (ancestor of Governor Samuel Ward)) who came to Newport and died there April 1698, æ 79; or she may have been the wife of Marmaduke Ward, another early settler. Jno. Ward is supposed, like Arthur Fenner, to have been in the Parliamentary Army. Another interesting fact brought to view in this will is, that Capt. Arthur had a son Samuel. He is nowhere else mentioned and must have died young.

WILL OF WILLIAM FENNER.

In the Name of God Amen.

I William ffenner Being very Sick and Weake In Body but of perfect Memory and vnderstanding and Knowing the

---

*Book 1—Council Records—Providence.

†In the year 1658, Nov. 22d, "William Fenner landed 5 Anchorr and a halfe of Liquors and one anker of wine" in Providence. The "anker" was a Dutch liquid measure formerly used in England and equal to ten wine gallons.

Certainty thatt I must Dye and Being Willing to Sett my house In Order Doe Make this my Last Will and Testamentt Nulling and Making void All former and Other Wills whatsoeuer.

IMP^s. I Comitt my Soul Into the Armes of Jesus Christ my Blessed Savior and Redeemer, and my Body to the Dust to be Desently Buried Att the Discretions of my Executors or either of them.

And after my Just Debts I Ow to any p^rson and ffuneral expenses be Justly and Truly P.id I Giue and Bequeath that Estate ye Lord hath giuen me As ffolloweth :

ITEM : I Giue and Bequeath that estate ye Lord hath giuen me As ffolloweth :

ITEM : I Giue and Bequeath to my Two Sisters Children viz: my Late Sister Lay her two Children She left and my Sister Phebe Ward ther Children Each of them twenty shillings a peece to be paid to them by my Executors In money or pay Equiuelent to money as they Shall Come to Age.

ITT^e. I Giue and Bequeath to my Brother Arthur ffenners two children Samuell and Phebe Venner, tenn pound a peece Besides an Equall Share of my whole Estate both of Lande and Chatles.

ITEM. I Giue and Bequeath my whole Estate (after my Debts and Legasces are paid to my two Brothers Children) Arthur and John ffenner, to be Equally Diuided Among them, and the Estate to be vallued at my Death and to Remaine In my Two Brothers hand till ther Children Come of Age, and as they Come of Age to be by them paid to there Children.

LASTLY. I make Ordaine and Appoint my Louing Brothers, Arthur And John ffenner Executors of this my Last Will and Testament In Testimony Whereof I haue herevnto Sett my Hand and Seale this : 30th : Day of August 1680.

Signed And published
In the presence of vs :
    Robert Carr
    John Williams

William ffenner

Robart Carr and John Williams appeared
before yᵉ Councill and attested the aboue
written to be yᵉ Last Will of William ffenner deceased and that he was in perfect
memory at yᵉ insealing and decleareing
thereof

Taken on their oathes in Councill this 6th
of September, 1680 p Natha'll Coddington
Clerk to yᵉ Coun'll

Placed on Record in
the 52 page of yᵉ
register of will yᵉ 20
of Septem'r 1680
pr Nath'll Coddington C : C

The following Deposition seems to have had special reference to the age of Capt. Arthur Fenner:

Whereas I Nath'll Goue, now inhabitant of Lebanon, in yᵉ year 1693,
begine to board at Capt. Arthur ffenner's House in Prouidence within
yᵉ Collony of Rhoad island and prouidence Plantations, And Lived
there about Eleven or Twelve year, in Which time I heard yᵉ Gentleman
tell Much of his comeing into yᵉ Country first and also of his Relations,
And in spetiall manner of his brother John ffenner That lived in Conet-
ticutt on yᵉ Great River at a place Called Potapogue ; some years after
I came to a place called Lebanon Where I am now. The 2d year after I
came, one Nath'll porter, formerly Desceased, had occasion to Go to
Killingworth to se a Childe of his at old Mr. Sam'll Benets and wold
have me to Go with him, Which also I did, And in our Travel wee Came
to yᵉ House of Capt. John ffenner, And in Discourse I told him That
he could not Go so Nimble as his Brother Arthur could he replyed he
was Lame I told That his Brother Arthur was yᵉ oldest Man as I always
understood, To yᵉ Which Capt John ffenner replyed and said that Arthur
was old enought to be his Father and said also that Arthur belonged to a
Troop of Horse under Lord Crumwell when he was a Boy.

Nath'll Goue

Connecticutt Ss^t   Lebanon,
Windham County Ss^d   March 29, 1743

Mr. Nath'll Goue The above Gamed Deponent personally appeared and
made Solemn Oath To the Truth of the foregoing Deposition, &c.,
Coram   Jon Trumble, Assis.
Justice of yᵉ peace, &c.

With reference to the burial place of the first Arthur Fenner, Mr. Pardon F. Brown furnishes the following further
information.

Aunt Polly Fenner, who lived with her brothers Benjamin and Samuel in the old Fenner Castle, the three constituting the last relics of that branch of the family, was a woman of very retentive memory and well versed in the traditions of the family. She strongly affirmed that a rough stone on the South East Corner of the ancient Maj. Thomas burying ground, near the site of the "castle" marks the grave of Capt. Arthur Fenner, the tomb stone of Maj. Thomas being found on the South west corner of the plat. Miss Polly Fenner was born Nov. 13, 1766, and died Sep. 14, 1861.

Since the first number of this Genealogy was issued the ancient chimney of the Capt. Arthur Fenner house, being found to be in a dangerous condition, has been pulled down and removed. The frontispiece of this number gives quite a correct view of the building as it once appeared.

SECOND GENERATION.

Children of Arthur[1] & Mehitable Fenner:

The order of birth is uncertain.

2—   I.   Thomas, born Oct. 27, 1652.

3—   II.   Arthur[2].

4— III.   Samuel, died young.

5— IV.   Freelove.

6—   V.   Bethiah,

7— VI.   Phebe.

8—VII.   Sarah, buried Nov. 7, 1676.*

There may have been other children who died young.

2.

Major Thomas Fenner, son of Capt. Arthur and Mehitable Fenner, born Oct. 27, 1652. He swore allegiance to the English government in May, 1671, about which time, being of age, he probably married. He undoubtedly married as his first wife Alice Ralph, daughter of Thomas Ralph, who was born Jan'y 13, 1657. An ancient town record in the Foster Mss., under date of the "11th of ye first month (March) 1676", makes mention of a son born to Tho. Fenner (that date). Thomas Ralph in his will mentions his grandson William Fenner, who could have been none other than son to Maj. Thomas. He died early, as he has no other record in the family history.

*See Town Record in Foster Mss.

Maj. Thomas was married, 2d, July 26, 1682, to Dinah Burden, [or Borden] born Oct. 1664, daughter of Thos. & Mary (Harris) Borden, by Joseph Jencks, assistant. During the time of the Indian war in 1676 Maj. Fenner was one who "staid and & went not away." Maj. Fenner became possessed of considerable property besides that inherited from his father's estate, who divided his land between his two sons.

There was laid out to him 1682 fifteen acres of land upon the right of Wm. Fenner; in 1687 fifty acres upon the original right of Jno. Lippitt; also in the same year six and a half acres on the right of Lippitt, and twenty acres upon the right of Jno. Sheldon of Pawtuxet, which land Arthur Fenner bought of him. These lands lay "adjoining to the land whereon the now Dwelling House of the aboue said Thomas ffenner standeth."

The house referred to was that built by him near the present Johnson line about a quarter of a mile west of his father's residence upon rising ground on the same side of the road. Part of this building with the original chimney remains as a fine historic relic of the past. This part, the end nearest the public highway, has inscribed high up on the chimney the date when it was first built, 1677. The other end of the house was rebuilt in 1835. The old chimney measures on the outside thirteen feet and two inches in width. On the inside the size has been curtailed by the building of an inner wall of brick. It was originally eight feet wide, four feet deep and five feet high. The chimney with its ancient trammels and pot-hooks opens its generous space into the one "great room", where Maj. Fenner, as justice, held his court, and where the immense girders about the ceiling, and the summer or central floor timber above still speaks of "ye olden tyme."

Maj. Fenner gave frequent notice of courts "to be held in his new house in Providence Woods", and evinced conscientiousness and high sense of honor in the decisions he reddered.*

This ancient edifice is in a fine state of preservation, and has been occupied successively by Major Thomas Fenner, his son Hon. Joseph Fenner, James Fenner, (who inherited it from his grandfather Joseph), and Thomas Fenner, his son in company with his step-father, Job Sheldon. Since then it has descended to the Joy and Hazard families who are in the Fenner line. Samuel Joy, himself a descendant of Capt. Fenner, occupied this house till his death in July, 1881. A good representation of this build ing is given in the frontispiece.

Major Fenner had a sixty acre lot lying near "Hipse's Rock", in the lands of Pawtuxet, containing eighty-eight and one-half acres by standard measure, and also fifteen acre lot containing eighteen and three quarters acres. Sept. 20, 1708, he addressed a communication to the purchasers and proprietors of Providence with reference to the running a line midway between the Pawtuxet River and the Wonasquatucket as far as Hipse's Rock.

June 26, 1701, Stephen Williams for £80 deeded to Thos. Fenner one-half part of a farm of upland swamp and meadow containing three hundred acres upon and adjoining to Neutaconkonett hill, bounded north by land of John Thornton, east by land of Arthur Fenner, Sen., and on the west partly by land of Thos. Fenner and partly with the common, with one-half part of houses thereon.

27 March, 1703, Zachariah Jones for five pounds deeded to Thos. Fenner one-eighth part in all the lands lying on the western side of Pocasset River, called Pawtuxet lands.

Nathaniel Thomas of Marshfield sold to Thomas Fenner

*A paper illustrating his sensitive regard for duty with reference to the marriage of Edward Potter in 1711 with Jane, the widow of his deceased brother John might be quoted. The old question of the legality of such a marriage and the kindred union of a man with his deceased wife's sister was a troublesome one then as it has been since in England. Major Thomas refused to marry them and they married themselves in a kind of Quaker style.

and Daniel Abbott in the year 1713 for £100, one fourteenth part of undivided land belonging to the proprietors of Pawtuxet in the thirteenth purchase. Ninety acres of land was laid out April 1, 1710 to Thomas Fenner on the east side of the seven mile line at a place called Sukahankanot, partly on the original right of Wm. Fenner, and partly on that of John Lippitt.

Maj. Fenner is said to have had about four hundred and fifty acres, which he distributed among his family.

Maj. Thomas was a valuable citizen, a faithful public officer, and exerted a wide influence in the Providence Plantations, being also very active in colonial affairs.

He was a Deputy in 1683, '91, '95, '97, '99, 1704 and 1705. He was in the Town Council quite frequently between the years 1698 and 1706. He held the office of Governor's Assistant 1707, '8, '9, '10, '11, '12, '13, '15, '16 and '17. In 1712 he held the commission of "Major for the Main."

On the 22d of February, 1714-5 Maj. Thomas entered into an agreement with his brother Arthur Fenner concerning the division of the lands of their father on the west side of the seven mile line. The former was to have all the original right of land which was their uncle William Fenner's, and Arthur was to have all the original right which belonged to his father.

Maj. Fenner died Feb. 27, 1718, ae. 65 years and 5 months, his will having been made Feb. 19, of same year.

In this document he makes due provision for his wife Dinah, and his "poor helpless child Eleazar," bestows £5 apiece on his three daughters Freelove Westcotte, Mehitable Starkweather, and Mary Abbott, and divides his remaining property between his five sons Thomas, Richard, Joseph, Arthur and John.

His inventory of personal property amounting to £433. 19. 09.*

---

*In his inventory are enumerated 8 pewter plates, 10 porringers, 2 quart potts, a pint pott, and pewter cup. Also 24 spoons, one silver spoon and a silver cup, (the latter two, great rarities in that period). These with several books, warming pan, 3 brass kettles, and 5 chairs, two horses, and 4 mares and a youngling colt, 15 cows, a bull, 26 young cattle, 8 swine, showed a large degree of wealth. His instruments of surveying indicated that he followed closely in the steps of his father.

Mrs. Dinah Fenner died Dec. 18, 1761, in her 98th year. Their tombstones together with that of their son Eleazer, may be found with others recording the deaths of their descendants in the old Fenner graveyard, near the ruins of Capt. Arthur's "castle," not far from the Pochassett River. Mrs. Dinah Fenner's gravestone has the following obituary upon it.

"During the course of a long life she praecuised all the relative Duties and died a SINCERE CHRISTIAN." What better could have been her eulogy.

Child of Thomas and Alice Fenner:

9. William.—probably the son born March 11, 1676, who evidently died young.

Children of Major Thomas and Dinah Fenner:

10. I. Mehitabel, m. 1st, Timothy Starkweather: 2d, Samuel Sterry ; 3d, Dr. Wm. Blodgett. f.

11. II. Freelove, m, Samuel Westcott. f.

12. III. Thomas, m. 1710, Mary Abbott. f.

13. IV. Mary, b. 1692, m. Daniel Abbott. f.

14. V. Joseph, b. 1693, m. 1st, Wait Harris; 2d, Amy Kinnicut. f.

15. VI. Richard, b. 1695, m. 1st, Abigail Sheldon ; 2d, Abigail Thornton. f.

16. VII. Sarah, b. 1698, m. 1st, Dr. John Jenckes; 2d, William Antram.

17. VIII. Arthur, b. Oct. 17, 1699, m. Mary Olney. f.

18. IX. Eleazar, b. Sept. 4, 1702, unmarried, d. July 31, 1723.

19. X. John, b. Sept. 16, 1705, unmarried. He was a Captain ; died Oct. 12, 1725, æ 20. The two last are buried in the Maj. Thomas burying ground.

3

Arthur Fenner, son of Capt. Arthur (1), married Mary Smith, dau. of John Smith, the Miller, and his wife Sarah.

He is spoken of as a yeoman, followed agricultural pursuits, and seems to have attained no celebrity. Many of his descendants have resided in the town of Cranston, and have been esteemed as useful citizens. He lived in the township of Providence in the house erected by his father, and died April 24, 1725. His inventory amounted to £411-19-0, his will having been made July 23, 1723. She made her will May 30, 1728, and died Dec. 13, 1737.

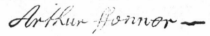

Children:

20. 1. Mary, died unmarried, Oct. 7, 1745.
21. II. Marcy, m. Oct. 13, 1726, Solomon Solomon Rutenburg. f.
22. III. Arthur, m. ——— f.
23. IV. John, m. Nov. 1, 1724, Amy Colwell. f.
24. V. Edward, m. Apr. 11, 1728, Amy Thornton. f.

The step-mother of Arthur Fenner, Jr., Mrs. Howlong Fenner, executed a curious legal document in favor of Arthur her *son in-law* (the ancient term for step-son) in the year 1706, which is subjoined, with his guarantee:

"Howlong ffenner of Providence, widdow & Relique of yᵉ captain Arthur ffenner for naturall love unto my well beloved son-in-law Arthur ffenner, &c. give to him all my household Goods Two Bedds the one a ffeather Bedd the other Bedd mixed with fieathers & fflocks with all the ffurniture & Beddsteds belonging to yᵉ Bedds And a Truʌke, a Chest, two Boxes with all that they containe; Two Brass Kettells, Two Iron Kettells, Two Iron Potts, a Brass Pann, a warmeing pann, a ffrying pann, a spitt & a Dripping pann, with all my Pewter, & a Steele & a Gunn of, seven foote Barrill; with three Trammills, two pair fire Tongs, a Gridd Iron a Fire Peile, with all other household Goods of wood or any Cask whatsoever or moveable estate that shall be found, &c." 16th March, 1705-6.

Arthur ffenner in a document, recorded after the above, agrees, "that if my said mother-in-law in case she shall see cause to demand all ye whole estate in ye deede specified at any time, then shall said deede be delivered & of no account more than any other wast paper : otherwise to stand in full force and power : And further to be understood that my Mother-in-law shall from time to time & at all times use any part for her owne use without any hindrance during her naturall life. In witness whereof, &c."

Signed 16th Mar., 1705-6 by Arthur ffenner. Recorded Dec. 31, 1708 by Thos. Olney, Clerk.

In the year 1717-18, Feb. 7, Maj. Thomas Fenner deeded to his brother Arthur all the goods which his honored uncle Wm. Fenner of Potapogue, Conn., deceased, did by his last will and testament give unto him the said Arthur Fenner.

5

FENNER—CRAWFORD.

Freelove Fenner, daughter of Capt. Arthur, married April 13, 1687, Gideon Crawford. He was a relative of Gov. John Cranston, and according to Theodore Foster, Esq., came to this country from Scotland on account of that relationship, both being descendants from James Lindsay, the first Earl of Crawfurd, his family having taken this name when the Earldom of Crawfurd was created by King Robert II in 1399. The sepulchre of this family is in the Grey Friars of Dundee. The ancestry is greatly distinguished in Scottish history. Gideon Crawford, coming to Providence about 1685, engaged in commercial enterprises which brought wealth to himself and family. He engaged in the West India trade, sending out some of the first vessels from this port. He died Oct. 10. 1707. His will* mentions his wife and two brothers-in-law and his cousin Richard Waterman, Jr. He left a large estate for that period. His widow

Page 161, Vol. 1, Prov. Rec.

carried on the business concerns left by her husband with great energy, accumulating a large property. She made her will June 1, 1712, and died at that date. Her inventory of real and personal property showed her to be possessed of ample means. They were buried in the North Burial Ground.

Children of Gideon and Freelove Crawford :

25. I. William, b. April 12, 1688, m. Sarah Whipple. He d. 1720. He left a large estate, his inventory amounting to £3,551 : 19 : 1d, being the largest that had been yet exhibited in Providence.

26. II. Anne, b. May 13, 1690, m. Nov, 29, 1711, Peleg Carr.

27. III. John, b. Aug. 1693, m. Dec. 20, 1715, Amey Whipple. He built the "Crawford House" still standing* west of the old Canal market. His ships were launched near his house. He died Mar. 18, 1718–19, and his personal inventory amounted to £1614–02–11†. He owned several vessels, besides real estate, and was accustomed to a luxurious style of living.

28. IV. Mary, b. Sept. 14, 1702, m. Oct. 12, 1724, James Mitchell.

FENNER—KILTON.

6

Bethiah Fenner, daughter of Capt. Arthur and Mehitable Fenner, m. Robert Kilton. Children :

29. I. Thomas, b. Jan. 17, 1690, m. Sept. 13, 1716, Phebe Dexter, dau. Stephen ; (had children : Free- love, Joseph, Thomas, William and Stephen.)

30. II. Samuel, b. ———— ———, m. Anne Harris, dau. Nicholas.

July 31, 1688, Arthur Fenner executed a deed of gift to his three daughters, Freelove, Bethiah and Phebe, constituting

*Dorr's Planting of Providence, p. 54.
†Prov. Probate Rec. Vol. 2.

a tract of thirty-four acres, lying in Providence Neck. On the 15th August, 1688, Phebe Fenner sold her part of the property to Gideon Crawford (her brother-in-law) for £10.

14th Dec. 1691, Walter Clark, of Newport, as administrator on estate of Thomas Sucklin, deeded to Capt. Arthur Fenner a town right of five acres, bounded north by land of Robert Kelton, west and south by highway, east by land of Henry Browne, together with commonage, for the sum of £5, to be paid for the use of the people called Quakers in said island. This towne right was passed over by Capt. Fenner to his son-in-law, Robert Kilton, on 25th Feb 1702. The above indicates where the residence of Robert Kilton was.

FENNER–LATHAM.

7

Phebe Fenner, daughter of Capt. Arthur and Mehitable
    Fenner, m. Joseph Latham. They lived in
    Saybrook, Conn. The date of his will was
    Nov. 24, 1705. Children :

31. I. Robert, never married.
32. II. Sarah, never married.
33. III. Phebe, m. March 12, 1727, John Martin.

THIRD GENERATION.
STARKWEATHER.—STERRY.—BLODGETT.

10.

Mehitabel Fenner, daughter of Maj. Thomas (2), grand-
    daughter of Capt. Arthur (1), married 1st,
    Timothy Starkweather. She m. 2d, Samuel
    Sterry, and removed to Preston, Conn. He
    d. Oct. 9, 1737. She m. 3d, Dr. Wm. Blodgett.

Children of Timothy and Mehitabel Starkweather :

34. I.   Samuel.
35. II. Joseph.
36. III. Arthur, killed by lightning.
37. IV. Mehitabel, m. Jan. 25, 1745, John Birket.
38. V. Mary,

Child of Samuel and Mehitabel Sterry :

39. Roger, who was town clerk in Preston, Conn.

Jan. 10th. 1732, Samuel and Mehitabel Sterry, gave a re ceipt to their brothers Richard and Joseph.Fenner, executors of the last will of their father, Maj. Thomas Fenner, for the property which fell to their portion.

WESTCOTT,

II.

Freelove Fenner, daughter of Maj. Thos. (2), granddau. of Capt. Arthur (1), m. Samuel Westcott, son of Jeremiah, grandson of Stukeley, born about 1678. His inventory taken Mar. 21, 1716. He died Mar. 17, 1716. She m. 2d, —— Stone. [See Deed given by her to her brothers Richard and Joseph, Dec. 25, 1749. She received seventy pounds for her portion from her brothers. Johnston Rec. Bk. 1, p. 178.]

Children:

40. I. Samuel, b. Jan. 24, 1704; m. Mary——. She was b. Nov. 28, 1703.

41. II. Jabez. m. Martha Edwards.

42. III. Freelove.

43. IV. Thomas, m. Elizabeth. He died 1772.

44. V. Benjamin, (prob.) m. 1733, Mary Carpenter.

45. VI. Jeremiah, m. Dec. 8, 1747, Freelove Bennett; d. prior to 1762.

June 29, 1727, Jabez Westcott signed a receipt to his uncle Joseph Fenner for the property left by his father. July 4, 1732, Thomas Westcott signed a receipt to his uncle Joseph Fenner for his share of his father's property. Johnston Records.

12.

Thomas Fenner, son of Maj. Thomas, (2) grandson of Capt. Arthur. (1)

He married, 1710, Mary Abbot, daughter of Daniel Abbott, High Sheriff, and sister of Gov'r Daniel Abbott.

Children:

46 I. Thomas, m. 1st, Phebe Hawkins. She d. Mar. 6, 1750. 2d, Sarah Warner. She d. April 20, 1751. 3d, Freelove Turner. f.

47. II. William, m. Christian Arnold. f.
48. II. Daniel, b. 1710, m. (1) Sept. 24, 1732, Jane Roberts,
     dau. Wm. she was b. 1712 and d. Feb. 17,
     1762. m. (2) Oct. 3, 1762, Sarah Haines, dau.
     William. f.
49. IV. Mary, Ephraim Bowen. f.

The father gave his sons Thomas and Daniel 60 acres
land, Oct. 17, 1744.

ABBOTT.

13.

Mary Fenner, daughter of Maj. Thomas, (2) granddaugh-
ter of Capt. Arthur (1), b. 1692, m. Hon. Daniel Abbott,
son of Daniel and Margaret Abbott, b. 1682, He was Deputy Governor. They had no children. She died Jan. 7,
1759, He died Nov. 7, 1760, having mads his will July 2d,
of that year, with codicil Sept. 15th, leaving most of his
property to his Fenner relatives. He provided for his
nephew Thomas Fenner the avails of his farm in Providence,
then in the occupation of James Hoyle, being given to him
for his support during his natural life. To the children of
his nephew Thomas Fenner, viz : Abbott and Antram, and
those of his nephew Daniel, viz : Samuel, Daniel and Thomas, and to those of his nephew William, viz : William and
Stephen, and to Jabez and Oliver Bowen, sons of his neice
Mary, Gov. Abbott left all his houses, lands, tenements and
real estate to be equally divided amongst them, They were
both buried in the North Burial Ground.

14.

Hon. Joseph Fenner, son of Maj Thomas, (2) grandson
of Capt. Arthur, (1) born 1693, married 1st Wait Harris,
daughter of Thomas Harris[3], and sister of Henry Harris,
Esq. She was born Apr. 21, 1694. She d. —— He m.
2d, Mar. 26, 1758, Mrs. Amy Kinnicutt, widow of Capt.
Roger Kinnicutt. He died June 22, 1779 in his 87th year.
His second wife died June 22, 1782, age 67 years and 5
months. He is spoken of by his cotemporaries as "conspic-
uous for a virtuous upright conduct which ever attracts the

attention and ensures the esteem of a free people." "He did
not escape the solicitations of his country to serve in
stations of public trust; he was chosen a representative for
the town of Providence in the General Assembly, which
place having filled with ability and integrity, to his own
honor and the satisfaction of the public, he was afterwards, in the year 1726, elected by the freemen at large a
member of the Governor's Council, to which he belonged
until 1740, but being fond of a life of quietness and retire-
ment, free from the noise and trouble of the political world,
he that year resigned his place at the Council Board, when
his brother Richard Fenner, Esq. was chosen in his room."
In 1725-6 he is spoken of on the records as lieutenant.

Joseph Fenner lived and died in the old homestead of his
father, his brother Richard probably residing for a time there
with him. This was near Simmonsville Factory, on the left
hand side of the road on the hill going west.

Children of Joseph and Wait Fenner:

50   I.   Mehitabel, b, Jan. 22, 1717, m. Southgate (or Cir-
          cuit) Langworthy of Newport. She d. Dec.
          19, 1744.
51. II. Thomas, b. Dec. 8, 1719, m. (1) widow Mary
          Cloyn, (2) Marcy Sheldon.   f.
52. III. Phebe, b. Dec. 11, 1725, m. Dr. Benjamin Slack of
          Scituate.   f.
53   IV. Joseph, b. Feb. 26, 1728, d. unmarried, æ 20.
54. V.   Wait, b. June 9, 1733, m. Sept. 25, 1755, Benj.
          Spencer* of E. Greenwich. S. P.
55. VI. Asahel, b. Nov. 8, 1737, m. Rhobe Sarle. He d.
          1777.   f.

In his will dated May 18, 1774, Joseph Fenner mentions
his wife Ammey, his daughter-in-law Robe, wife of Asahel
Fenner, dec., his two grandsons James and Joseph Fenner,
sons of Asahel and his other eight grandchildren by name.

In a memorandum left among his papers we find "7th of

---

*Another account says Sprague,

January, 1748, then my poor grandchild became blind with both eyes."

Joseph Fenner united with his brother Richard, April 18, 1722, in carrying out the wishes of their father in the matter of a division of property that Maj. Thomas had held in common with Nicholas Harris. In the division a dwelling house standing upon one part of said land had fallen to Thomas Fenner, and it was agreed betwixt them that Nicholas Harris should have four acres and one-half more in the division of said tract, but there being no instrument drawn in the lifetime of Thomas Fenner, the sons employed Andrew Harris, surveyor, to lay out and complete the same, reference being made to the plat of the same, by which it appears that Nicholas Harris' part contained one hundred and seventy-seven acres, and Thomas Fenner's one hundred and nine acres.

The final division of Capt. Arthur Fenner's estate was made Feb. 27, 1735-36, between Richard Fenner and Joseph Fenner, sons of Major Thomas, deceased, on the one part, and Edward Fenner, son of Arthur Fenner,[2] Esq., deceased, and John Thornton and John Manton, guardians to Mary Fenner, daughter of John Fenner, deceased, son of said deceased Arthur Fenner[2]. An agreement had been made between the two sons of Capt. Arthur, but it was not fully carried out till the above date, when a line having been run northward and southward across the homestead farm, the one hundred and nine and a quarter acres to the eastward of said line were assigned to the heirs of Arthur Fenner[2], being land lying mostly upon the southern or southwestern part of Neutaconkanut Hill, with part of the farm that formerly belonged to Joseph Wise, and an equal portion on the west side of said line to belong to the heirs of Major Thomas.

15.

Hon. Richard Fenner, son of Thomas (2), grandson of Capt. Arthur (1), born 1695. He was m. 1st, Jan. 11, 1716, to Abigail. daughter of Nicholas and Abigail (Tillinghast) Sheldon, by Richard Brown, Justice. He m. 2d, widow Abigail Thornton, daughter of Richard Clemence. He lived probably for a time in the old homestead and then built near the spot now occupied by the Simmons mansion in Johnston. The old house was moved back to its present position some years since, and has been somewhat changed in its appearance. He was appointed Justice of the Peace by Gov. Wanton for the town of Providence, in 1732, and held various offices of honor. By his will made Sept. 8, 1772, it appears that his wife survived him. He died 1773, aged about 78.

In his will Richard Fenner, Sen'r, left his wife in care of his son Arthur. giving his daughter Lydia £100 and various articles of furniture. To his sons Richard and Jeremiah he bequeathed all his right in that tract of land belonging to his brother Joseph and himself a little southeasterly of the hill called Chaupaumeskock Hill. To his son John he gave all the right of his brother Joseph and himself in a tract in Glocester. Upon his son Arthur, whom he constituted executor, he bestowed his homestead farm in Johnston and his right in the undivided lands within the propriety of Pawtuxet. His inventory of personal property amounted to £330-4-9½.—[Johnston Prob. Rec. Vol. 1, p. 87.

Children (not in exact order):

56. I. Abigail, born 1716, died before father.
57. II. Richard, born about 1718, m. Elizabeth Arnold. f. He died Feb. 17, 1799.
58. III. Lydia, born about 1720, m. Job. Angell, b. 1718.
59. IV. Arthur, born Jan. 6, 1725, m. Phebe Harris. f. He died Feb. 7, 1793.
60. V. John, m. Ruth Potter.
61. VI. Jeremiah, born 1730, m. Anne Warner. He died Feb. 12, 1789.

JENCKS—ANTRAM.

16.

Sarah Fenner, daughter of Thomas (2), grandson of

Capt. Arthur, (1) b. 1698, m. 1st Dr. John Jenckes, son of Governor Jenckes, Mar. 22, 1721. Dr. Jenckes died probably on board ship returning from England where he had been on a visit with his father.

She m. 2d, Wm. Antram. She d. April 17, 1736, in 39th year of her age.

Children (by 1st m.) *Jenckes.*

62. Lydia, m. Jonathan Jenckes.

63. Joseph.

64. Benjamin.

65. Mary, b. 1721. d. Nov. 14, 1723, buried in Major Thomas' burying ground.

Children (by 2d m.) *Antram.*

66. Sarah, m. May 26, 1750, Darius Sessions, Esq.

67. William.

Wm. Antram, senior, and Wm. Antram, Jun'r, distillers, for £1000 paid by Richard and Joseph Fenner, quit-claim to them, equally to be divided between them all their right and title which they had in and to all the estate, both lands goods, chattells which of right belonged to John Fenner. dec'd, or that might have been lawfully claimed by him in virtue of the last will and testament of his honored father, Major Thomas Fenner, provided that said John Fenner had lived to attain to the age of twenty-one. This document is found in Vol. 12, Prov. Records, p. 371, and is dated Feb. 26. 1750.

17.

Hon. Arthur Fenner, son of Major Thomas, (2) grandson of Capt. Arthur, (1) b. Oct. 17, 1699. He was m. 1st, June 2, 1723, to Mary Olney, daughter of Capt. James and Hallelujah Olney, by James Jenckes, Deputy Governor. She d. Mar. 18, 1750, age 54 years, 5 months, and 18 days. He married 2d, Barbara ——, who survived him,

He lived in the town of Providence. He was in the early part of his life, before the division of the state into three counties, which happened in he year 1729, employed in the executive part of the government; and afterwards as a Jus-

tice of the Peace. He was a merchant of eminence, and
for a long time was a member of the Baptist church.

The great change wrought in the lapse of centuries is
strikingly illustrated by the following, from the writings of
John Howland, as quoted by Stone. Between the home of
the Fenners and the site of this city was in early times a
populous Indian villiage near Mashapaug pond.

"The venerable Arthur Fenner, the grandfather of Gov.
James Fenner was born in Cranston in the year 1699, twen-
ty-three years after the close of Philip's war, and he has in-
formed me that when a young man, on travelling the road
from his father's house to town, it was usual to pass more
Indians than white people on the way."

Sept. 27, 1721, Richard and Joseph Fenner, executors of
their father's will, signed an agreement making a partition
of the estate of their father, Hon. Thomas Fenner, assign-
ing their brother Arthur, "that house and tenement lying in
Providence, which their father purchased of Capt. Silvanus
Scott, bounding north and east with lands of Capt. Waterman, and south with lands of Daniel Abbott and on the
west with the Towne Street ; and also two six acre lots adjoining together and lying in the neck on the backside of
said town, lying between the land of Capt. Whipple on the
south, and land of Wm. Field on the north, a highway on
the west side, and the sea or salt River of Pawtucket on
the east."

The same parties in a document dated Nov. 13, 1763, recorded on Johnston Records, Nov. 22d, jointly made a confirmatory deed to their brother Arthur, having paid to him,
Aug. 31, 1726, sixty pounds in money in part of his portion,
with "the lot and housing in Providence Town where our
said brother Arthur now dwells—secondly, two six acre lots
in Providence Neck with a thatch cove adjoining called
Wachear Cove—thirdly one whole lot and a half in the
Stated Common Division in Providence which may be found
in the general plan of the said stated common lots which
derived from that right and a half which belonged to our said

father—fourthly, about ninety-one acres and a half standard measure lying in the township of Smithfield a small
distance easterly from the dwelling place of Job Angell or
by the return thereof may show—fifthly, about three hundred and thirty-two acres and a half standard measure at
a place called Suckatunkneck, within the township of Johnston—sixthly, one hundred and forty acres of land lying nigh
to that place where John Abslonn formerly lived in the
township of Scituate."

His first wife is spoken of in glowing terms by a relative
of the family. "She was one of the smart and active wom-
en of her time. She was a merchant and owned more navi-
gation than any other person in town ; acquired the estate,
kept a store and shop and maintained the family in affluence.
She bought vessels and cargoes. Her husband for many
years was sickly and unable to do business. She had
twelve children."

He died Feb. 2, 1788, age 88. His funeral was attended
at his mansion house,where a sermon was preached by Elder
Mitchell, and his remains were interred in the North Burying Place.

A "History of the Bible" owned by him and supposed to
be inherited from his grandfather, Capt. Arthur, is in the
possession of his descendant, Mr. A. F. Dexter, who lives
on the old Fenner place at What Cheer.

Children of Arthur and Mary (Olney) Fenner:

68. I.   Freelove, born August 25, 1723, died young.
69. II.   Sarah, born September 10, 1725, died young.
70. III. John, born April 17, 1727, died young.
71. IV.   James, b. Feb. 9, 1730, m. Freelove Whipple.   f.
72. V.   Arthur, born October 12, 1732, died young.
73. VI.   Joseph, born Nov. 8, 1734, died Nov. 17, 1751.
74. VII. Mary, born May 15, 1737, m. E. Rumreill.   f.
75. VIII. John, born October 2, 1739, m. Phebe Brown.
76. IX.   Sarah, April 28, 1741, died January 3, 1756.
77. X.   Freelove, born July 13, 1743, m. Simon Smith.   f.

78. XI. Arthur, b. Dec. 10, 1745 (Governor) m. Amey
         Comstock. f.
79. XII. Lydia, born March 1, 1748, m. Hon. Theodore
         Foster. f., the accomplished Town Clerk of
         Providence, Member of Congress, etc.

RUTENBERG.

21

Mary Fenner, dau. of Arthur (3), grandson of Arthur (1).
         She m. Oct. 13, 1726, Solomon Rutenburg.
         Children :
80. 1. Thomas, m. Anne Westcott, daughter of Thomas.
81. II. Daughter, m. (1) Solomon Bradford. (2) Abel Pot-
         ter.
82. III. Daughter.

22

Arthur Fenner, son of Arthur (3), grandson of Capt. Ar-
         thur (1), m. probably Abigail, daughter John
         Dexter, who afterwards married Elisha Greene.
         She was born April 26, 1696. He died before
         his father. Child :
83. Sarah, married Dec. 24, 1738, Zachariah Mathewson.
         She was mentioned in her grandmother's will.

23

John Fenner, son of Arthur (2), grandson of Capt. Ar-
         thur (1), was m. Nov. 1, 1724, to Amey Col-
         well, dau. Robert Colwell and Amy, his wife,
         by Richard Brown Justice. He lived in Prov-
         idence, and died Nov. 24, 1725, intestate. His
         widow married (2) Joseph Thornton. Child :
84. Marcy (or Mary) born April 20, 1725. She was m.
         Oct. 6, 1743, to Seth Dean, of Plainfield, Ct.,
         by Richard Fenner, Esq., Assistant.

24

Edward Fenner, son of Arthur (3) grandson of Capt. Ar-
         thur (1), born

He lived in Cranston, R. I. He was a farmer.
On the 4th of Oct. 1756, it was represented to
the Town Council that Edward Fenner, Sen'r.,
was "Delirious and uncapable to transact and
manage his secular affairs and Buisness to the
great Hazzard and Damage of his Family and
Estate, Whereof on proof being made, Josiah
Thornton was appointed guardian." This
guardianship, however, was only temporary
and was discharged Dec. 25, 1756.

Edward Fenner married 1st. Phebe Barton : 2d, [? Amey]
Borden, dau. Richard. An Edward Fenner
married April 11, 1728, widow Amey Thornton—perhaps she was the daughter of Richard
Borden above. He was appointed executor,
with Col. James Waterman, of Richard Borden's estate. He died intestate, 1767, and his
son Stephen took administration of the estate
Oct. 19. Children (order not known) :

85. Edward, married 1st, Dinah Potter, f ; 2d, Welthan
Colgrove. f.

86. Arthur (Capt.) m. Rachel Westcott. She was born
1738 ; died Feb. 16, 1803, in 66th year.

87. John, married Lydia Carpenter : perhaps went to Hop-
kinton.

88. Stephen, married Frances Corpe. f.

89. Sarah, married Col. John Waterman. f.

90. Alice, m. 1st, ——— Stephens : 2d, Col. Jno. Waterman.

91. Esther, married William Corpe.

92. Mary, m. —— Harrington.

93. Freelove, married March 20, 1746, Andrew Edmonds.

Providence, R. I.   J. P. ROOT.

CPSIA information can be obtained
at www.ICGtesting.com
Printed in the USA
BVHW030756311221
625096BV00016B/272